River Boy

Written by Kerrie Shanahan

Illustrated by Walter Carzon

Flying Start
to Literacy®

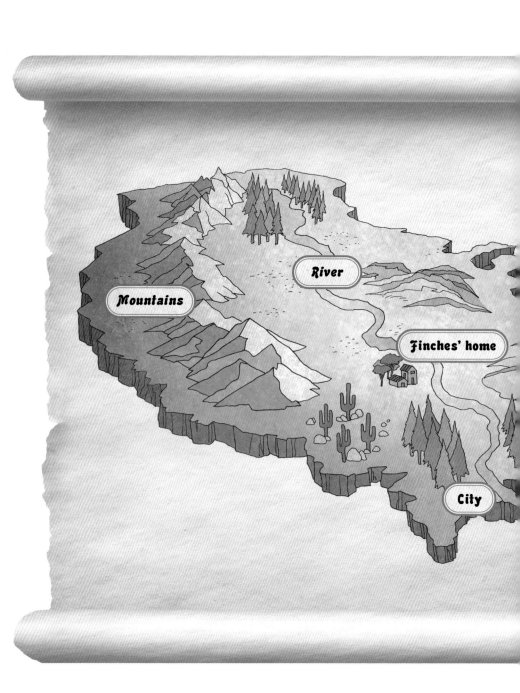

Mountains

River

Finches' home

City

Contents

Chapter 1

The river: friend and foe

"Here it comes," Charlie called out as he ran down the track to the port.

"Wait for me!" yelled Annie, as she pumped her six-year-old legs as fast as she could.

Charlie and Annie squinted into the sun as the large paddleboat drew closer. The graceful boat chugged along with its side paddle churning through the glistening water.

"One day, I'll be a paddleboat pilot." Charlie put his dream into words. "Just like Uncle Archie."

"Who's Uncle Archie?" asked Annie, looking up at Charlie.

"He's my uncle, and he drives paddleboats up and down the river," Charlie said proudly. "And when I'm old enough, I'll drive a paddleboat, too."

"Wow!" Annie was impressed. "You're 12 now. Is that old enough?"

"Almost," said Charlie thoughtfully.

They watched as the paddleboat stopped at the dock and the deckhands unloaded its cargo. Suddenly, Charlie felt a change in the air. A storm was on the way.

"Come on, Annie. We'd better get home, or your mum will be cross."

Charlie and Annie headed up the hill. They had a half-hour walk back to the Finch family farm on the outskirts of town, where Charlie lived with Mr and Mrs Finch and their children, Annie and Mack.

"Hurry, Annie. A rainstorm is coming." Charlie shuddered. He loved the river, but he knew it could also be a dangerous beast.

Charlie's mind drifted back to a frightening time eight years before, when the river turned from friend to foe. The year was 1885, and it had been raining solidly for days. The river had burst its banks and floodwaters were rising rapidly.

Charlie was young then, but he remembered snippets from that fateful day. He remembered the sky was as dark as night. He remembered the sound of torrential rain on the tin roof. And he remembered his mother and father taking him to the Finches' home.

"We'll be back soon, Charlie," they had said. "Be a good boy for Mrs Finch." Then they went back out into the ferocious storm.

Charlie later learnt that they had left to move their precious horses to higher ground. Sadly, they didn't return.

So, from that day on, Charlie was part of the Finch family.

Chapter 2

A shock for Charlie

Dinnertime at the Finches' was always noisy, with everyone wanting to share their news.

"Charlie and I saw a paddleboat today," Annie said loudly.

"I don't like them," said Mr Finch, shaking his head. "They're dangerous and unreliable."

"Father, paddleboats travel up and down the river quite often now," explained Mack. "And they're getting safer and faster."

"I'll stick to using rafts!" Mr Finch was definite. "I have always used a raft to get my goods to port and I see no reason to change."

"Charlie's going to be a paddleboat pilot when he's old enough," announced Annie.

Charlie's face coloured, and the whole family turned and looked at him.

Mr Finch laughed. "Well I'm not sure about that, but I do know Charlie's old enough to leave school."

Charlie looked up at Mr Finch, his eyes wide.

"Mack and I need your help on the farm, Charlie." Mr Finch's voice was serious. "Make tomorrow your last day, okay?"

Charlie groaned inwardly. He knew this day was coming, but he still wasn't ready for it. It wasn't that Charlie didn't want to help Mack and Mr Finch. He did and he was grateful to them, but he had a different idea about his future – he had always dreamt of being a paddleboat pilot, not a farmworker.

That night, Charlie couldn't sleep, so he crept out and sat next to the smouldering fire. His mind was racing.

I'm so thankful the Finches took me in after Mother and Father died. I even feel like a "real" Finch. But working on the farm? I don't like that idea. It makes Mack so tired, and he has no time for fishing or swimming anymore. But what choice do I have? I can't let Mr Finch down.

Then Charlie unfolded the treasured letter he'd received three years ago. He reread it for the thousandth time . . .

12th day of July, 1890

Dearest Charlie,

I think of you, my only nephew, with great fondness.
The sudden death of your parents five years ago
filled me with deep sorrow.

I know you are happy living with your kindly neighbours,
and I am forever grateful to them.

When the day comes, however, that you fancy
an adventure, be sure to find me. I am presently
learning the craft of paddleboat piloting a majestic
paddleboat on the river.

One day soon, I will be piloting my own paddleboat.

It would give me great pleasure to see you again.

Yours Sincerely,

Your loving uncle,

Archie Parsons

Chapter 3
A trip downstream

Charlie had been working on the farm for almost three weeks. It was hard work, tending crops of cotton, corn, potatoes and rice, and taking care of the fruit trees.

At the end of each day, he was exhausted, his back ached and his tender hands were sore and blistered.

And he missed the river. Charlie used to fish for catfish on his way home from school – Mrs Finch loved having fresh fish for dinner.

On hot summer evenings, he'd swim in the cool water. And he loved visiting the port in town to watch paddleboats moving up and down the river. He imagined what it might be like on board the grand boats.

One hot evening, Mr Finch was in a particularly good mood. "Lads, we've had a bumper crop this year, thanks to this fertile soil. We have enough left over from the harvest to sell. We'll take them to the city and try our luck."

"The city!" Charlie was excited. "I've always wanted to go there."

Mr Finch spent the next few days making a strong wooden raft for their trip.

It was a crisp morning as Mr Finch, Mack and Charlie set off on their trip to the city. They balanced on the wooden raft, with their cargo of crops piled high in the centre.

The current did the work as they floated along the river, using long poles to guide them. Mr Finch knew how to stay in the deep river channel, so as to avoid any snags or sandbars.

At times, when the wind eased, they moved slowly and gently along the smooth river. But in some places the river was treacherous, and the swift current moved their small raft around like a leaf in the wind. Mr Finch navigated safely through the small rapids and windy turns.

Charlie loved every bit of the raft trip. The vast, grand river, the wind in his hair, the sound of the water whooshing and gushing around him – and the feeling of freedom as they manoeuvred their way downstream.

After five days on the river, they reached the busy port in the city. A magnificent paddleboat was being unloaded and people milled around to watch.

Mack and Charlie unpacked their cargo and dismantled the wooden raft. Meanwhile, Mr Finch arranged sales for his crops and the timber from the raft.

Once the deals were done, Mr Finch was keen to get back home.

"Okay, lads. Let's go." And he set off briskly on the long trek home, with Charlie and Mack behind him.

"Mr Finch, I've been thinking," said Charlie. "It's such a big effort to build a raft. And we can use it only once because it can't go upstream against the current. Why don't you just put your crops on a paddleboat?"

"Paddleboats are too unreliable. They hit snags, run into sandbars, catch fire and blow up! I'll stick to what I know – thanks, Charlie." And that was that.

After ten long days of walking, they finally arrived back at the farm. It was somewhere during the long walk home that Charlie made a big decision.

Chapter 4

Charlie's difficult decision

One night before bed, Charlie got up the courage to speak to Mr and Mrs Finch.

"Thank you for having me in your home all these years." Charlie swallowed hard and he felt tears burning the back of his eyes.

Mrs Finch looked up from her sewing. "What are you trying to tell us, Charlie?"

"I've made a decision. It's time for me to leave. I'm going to find Uncle Archie and I'm going to become a paddleboat pilot." Charlie rattled off his thoughts in one long breath.

Mr and Mrs Finch were silent.

Then Mr Finch shook his head. "No, no, Charlie. How will you find your uncle? You don't know for sure that he's a paddleboat pilot."

"It's too dangerous!" said Mrs Finch, her voice filled with concern. "You must stay here. We're your family now."

"But it's what I've always dreamed of doing," Charlie said in a small voice, and his shoulders sank.

"You're too young," said Mr Finch. "You're just a boy. Now get some sleep. We have a big day tomorrow."

Charlie knew that there was no point in arguing. He loved the Finches, but it was time for him to set out on his own. He was going to stick to his plan. He was ready – he knew what he must do. He packed his bags before he went to bed.

Charlie slept lightly and woke before dawn. It was still dark outside, and the house was quiet as he silently crept into the kitchen. He placed a short but heartfelt note on the table.

I'm sorry everyone, but I have to follow my dream.

Thank you for everything.

Yours,

Charlie

Charlie held his breath as he opened the kitchen door . . .

"Charlie," a small voice whispered.

Charlie spun around. It was Annie.

"I heard you talking to Mother and Father. Please don't leave." Her eyes were filled with tears.

"I'm sorry, Annie, this is my dream," Charlie explained in hushed tones. "Now, go back to bed."

Annie hugged Charlie hard. "Will you come back?"

"One day I will," said Charlie. "I'll come back when I'm a paddleboat pilot." He took a deep breath before stepping out the door.

Chapter 5

A surprise for Charlie

The cold night air hit Charlie hard as he walked briskly away from his home. With each step, his heart felt heavier, and he could no longer stop the tears that welled up in his eyes. Like a flooded river breaking its banks, Charlie's tears overflowed. He walked on as he sobbed and sniffed.

As Charlie walked towards the river, he heard footsteps crunching on the gravel road behind him.

"Wait up, Charlie!" It was Mack.

"Mack? What are you doing here?"

"I heard you talking to Mother and Father, and I heard you leaving, so I followed you," said Mack.

"Really?" Charlie tried to hide his relief and smiled broadly.

Mack was coming with him. What a great adventure they would have!

"We're in luck, Mack," said Charlie, as they reached the wharf. A large paddleboat was there, loaded with cargo.

"Quick!" said Charlie. "We need to sneak on board, before it gets too light."

Mack didn't answer and he didn't move.

"What's wrong, Mack?" Charlie asked.

Mack hesitated. "Sorry, Charlie. I'm not going with you. I was never going with you."

"What do you mean?" Charlie wasn't expecting this.

"I wanted to ask you not to leave, but I can't. I know you have to try to find your uncle. But I can't come with you. Father would not be able to do all the farmwork without me," Mack explained. "It's just not right that I leave."

This news was a big blow to Charlie. He had liked the idea of having Mack with him.

"Quick, Charlie," Mack urged. "You'd better get on board."

"But?" Charlie was feeling nervous and unsure, and his mind raced. *Can I really do this? All by myself? Maybe I should go back to the farm, too.*

"Sorry, Charlie, but I have to get back home," said Mack. "Are you getting on the boat or coming with me?"

"Umm. I'll get on board," Charlie said quietly.

"Good for you, Charlie, and good luck!" Mack wasn't one for long goodbyes. He slapped Charlie on the back, turned on his heel and left.

Charlie watched as Mack headed back up the hill and out of sight.

The sun was rising and the boat would soon be leaving port. Charlie knew he had to get moving and find a good spot to hide. So with a pounding heart, he scrambled onto the grand paddleboat and headed straight to the back of the vessel.

He slipped in between some tall towers of cargo and found a nook to sit in. His plan was to get to the city downriver. It was a busy port, so surely someone there would know his uncle. All he needed was a bit of luck!

Chapter 6

A needle in a haystack

Charlie tucked himself behind the cargo and waited. Before long, the boat lurched forward, and Charlie was off on his adventure.

Hidden among the cargo, he felt a faint spray of water from the side paddle. And from his hiding spot, Charlie could see the riverbank – forests with large trees, steep jagged cliffs, and sugar and cotton crops. Occasionally, he saw people waving at the boat.

Charlie was tired, but he couldn't relax. *I must stay hidden,* Charlie thought.

But the chugging of the boat, the sun on his face and his sleepless night made Charlie drowsy. His eyelids grew heavy and he drifted off to sleep.

"What do we have here?" A loud voice jolted Charlie awake. He looked up and saw a hulking figure standing over him.

Charlie's heart sank. Was this the end of his dream?

"I'm Jack, the boat's cook." The large figure crouched down next to Charlie. "What are you doing here?"

Charlie stammered through his recount of how he came to be hiding on the paddleboat.

"So, where's this uncle?" asked Jack.

"I don't know," said Charlie. "But I need to find him."

"Sounds like you're looking for a needle in a haystacks." Jack laughed.

"I'd like to help you," said Jack. "But we can't have stowaways on the boat. I must tell the captain."

"Please don't tell!" Charlie was desperate. "I'll work for you. In the kitchen. *Please.*"

Jack thought for a moment. He liked the idea of some help.

"Okay," he sighed.

"Thank you!" Charlie was so relieved. His dream was still alive.

The rest of the three-day trip flew by. Charlie busily scrubbed pots and pans, peeled potatoes and washed dishes. Along the way, he struck up a friendship with Jack, the cheerful cook.

On the last morning of the trip, Charlie and Jack were cleaning the kitchen.

"We're almost at the end of our journey," Jack said. "And I have news about your Archie Parsons."

"Really?" Charlie was shocked.

"Yep. I've asked around on board, and Archie Parsons is piloting a paddleboat that's arriving later today."

"Wow! Thanks, Jack!"

"We're pulling into dock now," said Jack. "You'd better hide."

"Thanks for everything!"

Charlie dashed off and hid, and when no one was looking, he snuck off the boat.

Then he sat on the wharf and waited for the next paddleboat . . . and for Uncle Archie.

"Here comes the paddleboat!" the cry rang out. Charlie scanned the pilothouse as the paddleboat approached.

"There he is!" Charlie said, spotting the pilot guiding the huge vessel into the dock.

Charlie waited and waited. Finally, the paddleboat pilot came ashore. Charlie ran up to him.

"Uncle Archie!" Charlie grasped the pilot's arm.

"What do you want, kid? I'm not Archie. And I'm not your uncle." He shrugged Charlie's hand away and kept walking.

Charlie was devastated. He sat down on the edge of the wharf, with his head in his hands.

He had no idea what to do next.

"Charlie?" The voice made him look up. Through his tears, Charlie saw Jack, the cook, with his big familiar smile.

"Sorry it didn't work out," said Jack.

Charlie's shoulders slumped.

"What do you say?" asked Jack. "Do you want me to tell the captain that I've found a first-class kitchen hand? You could come back up the river with us."

Charlie's spirits immediately lifted. "Thanks, Jack. I'd really like that."

Charlie was disappointed that he didn't find Uncle Archie, but he wouldn't give up. And in the meantime, he was excited for more adventures on the river and maybe, one day, piloting his own paddleboat!

A note from the author

To write this historical fiction, I had to research life during the 1800s, when paddleboats were used to travel up and down rivers and along the coast. Life was tough back in these times, and people worked hard just to feed themselves and their families. Settlements were small but growing. The paddleboats brought an air of excitement to the river, but many people feared them. I used this information to make my story sound realistic.

When I was developing the character of Charlie, I wanted to show through his experiences and actions that he was brave, loyal, adventurous and kind.